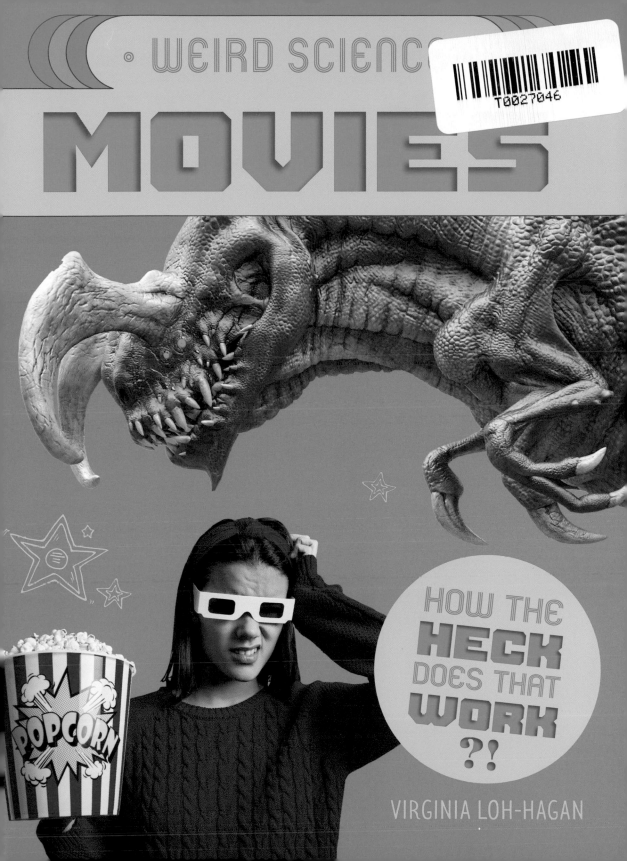

WEIRD SCIENCE

MOVIES

HOW THE HECK DOES THAT WORK ?!

POPCORN

VIRGINIA LOH-HAGAN

45TH PARALLEL PRESS

Published in the United States of America by Cherry Lake Publishing Group
Ann Arbor, Michigan
www.cherrylakepublishing.com

Reading Adviser: Beth Walker Gambro, MS, Ed., Reading Consultant, Yorkville, IL
Book Designer: Felicia Macheske

Photo Credits: © Hortimages/Shutterstock, cover, 1; © Krakenimages.com/Shutterstock, cover, 1; © DM7/ Shutterstock, cover, back cover, 1; © Melica/Shutterstock, back cover; © Drazen Zigic/Shutterstock, 4; © Bodor Tivadar/Shutterstock, 5; © AlinaMD/Shutterstock, 6; © Sareerat Phongsart/Shutterstock, 7; © Photo 12 / Alamy Stock Photo, 8; © Iryna Imago/Shutterstock, 10; © Dean Murray/Shutterstock, 11; © Gorodenkoff/Shutterstock, 12; © Yurii Andreichyn/Shutterstock, 14; © JJFarq/Shutterstock, 15; © Sergey Lavrentev/Shutterstock, 16; © WENN/Newscom, 18; © Marzufello/Shutterstock, 19; © Oldesign/Shutterstock, 19; © Buntoon Rodseng/ Shutterstock, 19; © Sarah Marchant | Dreamstime.com, 20; © Drawlab19/Shutterstock, 22; © dpa picture alliance / Alamy Stock Photo, 23; © Gemenacom/Shutterstock, 24; © Fine Art Studio/Shutterstock, 26; © CkyBe/ Shutterstock, 26; © Air Images/Shutterstock, 27; © Dmytro Zinkevych/Shutterstock, 28; © DC Studio/ Shutterstock, 30; © Suriya srion/Shutterstock, 31;

45th Parallel Press is an imprint of Cherry Lake Publishing Group.

Library of Congress Cataloging-in-Publication Data

Names: Loh-Hagan, Virginia, author.
Title: Weird science. Movies / by Virginia Loh-Hagan.
Other titles: Movies
Description: Ann Arbor, Michigan : Cherry Lake Publishing, [2021]
  | Series: How the heck does that work?! | Includes bibliographical references and
  index.
Identifiers: LCCN 2021005076 (print) | LCCN 2021005077 (ebook)
  | ISBN 9781534187634 (hardcover) | ISBN 9781534189034 (paperback)
  | ISBN 9781534190436 (pdf) | ISBN 9781534191839 (ebook)
Subjects: LCSH: Cinematography—Special effects—Juvenile literature. |
  Computer animation—Juvenile literature.
Classification: LCC TR858 .L64 2021 (print) | LCC TR858 (ebook) | DDC
  777—dc23
LC record available at https://lccn.loc.gov/2021005076
LC ebook record available at https://lccn.loc.gov/2021005077

Cherry Lake Publishing Group would like to acknowledge the work of the Partnership for 21st Century Learning, a Network of Battelle for Kids. Please visit *http://www.battelleforkids.org/networks/p21* for more information.

Printed in the United States of America
Corporate Graphics

Dr. Virginia Loh-Hagan is an author, university professor, and former classroom teacher. She's currently the Director of the Asian Pacific Islander Desi American Resource Center at San Diego State University. She loves watching movies, especially movies with Baby Yoda. She lives in San Diego with her very tall husband and very naughty dogs.

TABLE OF CONTENTS

INTRODUCTION 5

CHAPTER 1
STOP-MOTION 9

CHAPTER 2
CGI 13

CHAPTER 3
STUNTS 17

CHAPTER 4
SOUND EFFECTS 21

CHAPTER 5
3-D MOVIES 25

CHAPTER 6
STREAMING 29

GLOSSARY 32

LEARN MORE 32

INDEX 32

Movies can inspire people to change or take action.

INTRODUCTION

All kinds of weird science happen when making movies. Movies are motion pictures. They're stories recorded by cameras. They're shown in theaters or on television. Since the late 1890s, movies have entertained us. Movies have changed over the years. They've gone from silent to sound. They've gone from black and white to color.

People watch movies for all different reasons. They watch movies to be entertained. They watch movies to learn something new. They watch movies to laugh. They watch movies to cry.

There are many types of movies. There are drama movies. There are action movies. There are **animated** movies. Animation is when drawings are made to look like moving images.

In movies, the impossible seems possible. People fly. They climb on walls. They fight monsters. It can take days, months, and sometimes even years to make a movie. It takes a lot of different people to make a movie magical.

On a movie set, people do all sorts of jobs. They write the story. They act. They direct. They operate cameras. They edit films. They color films. They perform daring feats called **stunts**. They do lighting. They design costumes. They design sets. Today, technology helps make movie magic happen.

Dare to learn more about movie science! So much is going on. How the heck does it all work?

People all over the world make movies. People provide captions so viewers can understand the foreign language.

Stop-motion takes a long time. About 15 to 25 pictures make 1 second of screen time.

CHAPTER 1

STOP-MOTION

Do you like animated movies? What about monster movies? Some of these movies use stop-motion. Stop-motion is a process using models. These models can be puppets. They can be made of clay. They can be made of LEGO bricks. They can be drawings.

Models are placed in a scene. They're photographed. They're moved a little. Then, they're photographed again. This process is repeated many times. There are a lot of still images. These photographs are put in order. They're made into a movie. They're viewed very quickly one after the other. This looks like motion.

Stop-motion videos can be made with any camera.
You can make stop-motion videos with your phones.

Stop-motion creates an **illusion**. Illusions are misleading images. When watching stop-motion, you're seeing many pictures. These pictures flash quickly before your eyes. Your brain tries to make sense of it. Your brain smooths out the images. You see a seamless motion instead of different images. Your eyes and brain can only process 30 to 60 separate images per second. Your brain holds images for less than a second. It fills in any missing pieces. You do this based on what you've already seen. This creates the illusion of motion.

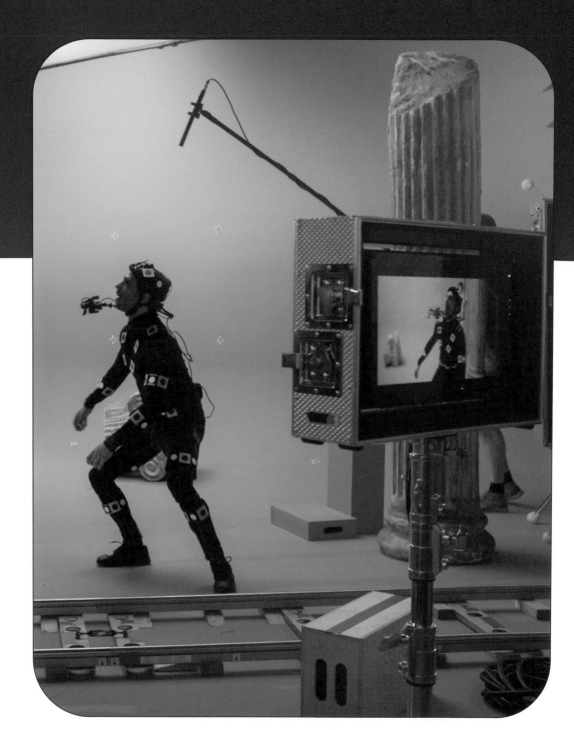

Today, many moviemakers use CGI more than stop-motion.

CHAPTER 2

CGI

What was the last action or fantasy movie you saw? These movies most likely used CGI. CGI means **Computer-generated** imagery. Computer-generated means to make something using a computer. CGI means computers make the images. CGI requires a lot of computer skills. People need to know how to use computer programs. CGI also requires art and design skills.

Computer **graphics** are created. Graphics are images. Computers create characters, scenes, and special effects. They create **three-dimensional** (3-D) models. 3-D means shapes don't look flat. 3-D models seem to pop out. They seem real.

Even
WEiRDER
MOVIE SCIENCE!

- In the past, movie studios made movies on reels. They sent these reels to movie theaters. Today, movie theaters use digital video projectors. They send movies through the internet, satellite, or hard drive. They use DLP technology. DLP means Digital Light Processing. Little mirrors are used to reflect light and color onto a screen.

- Film colorists color in the lines. After a movie is shot, colorists use editing software. They adjust colors. They adjust contrast. They add color to movies. They correct color mistakes. Sometimes, there's bad lighting. Colorists fix it by correcting the colors. They make all the scenes match.

- *The Wizard of Oz* had problems with makeup. Buddy Ebsen was the first actor to play the Tin Man. His make-up was made of aluminum powder. It coated his lungs. He had to go to the hospital and quit the movie. Margaret Hamilton played the Wicked Witch. She wore green makeup. The makeup caught on fire. She had burns on her hands and face.

CGI brings the graphics to life. Creators pay special attention to details. They focus on colors and lighting. They focus on **textures**. Texture means how something feels. Details are important. They're the key to making images look real. The CGI images are dropped into the movie. They have to blend in.

Movies require viewers to suspend their disbeliefs. This means viewers let themselves believe something is true even while knowing it's not. Good CGI keeps viewers watching the movie. Bad CGI pulls viewers out of the movie. The images look fake.

CGI is used in movies, TV, and video games.

Many dangerous stunts are done with CGI.

CHAPTER 3

STUNTS

Have you ever tried a stunt? Many movies have stunts. They show car crashes. They show falls from great heights. They show fight scenes and explosions. These stunts are most likely performed by stunt actors.

Stunt actors are trained professionals. Many go to special schools. They serve as **body doubles** for movie stars. This means they stand in for movie stars. Movie studios don't want their movie stars to get hurt. Also, movie stars most likely don't have the skills to do stunts. They just act like they do. Stunt actors step in for them. They do the real work.

Moviemakers work to maintain the illusion of stunts. **Production** is the time when the movie is being filmed. During production, moviemakers film bodies and stunts at certain angles. They never film the stunt actors' faces. They only film the movie stars' faces.

Post-production refers to the work done after a movie is filmed. During post-production, moviemakers make edits. They may **superimpose** the movie stars' faces onto stunt actors' bodies. Superimpose means to layer on top of something else.

In some cases, safety gear is used for stunts. In post-production, this gear is edited out. This can be done with CGI.

Stunt actors have to dress and act like their movie star doubles.

UNSOLVED MYSTERY

Bruce Lee is a martial arts legend and actor. At age 32, he died from brain swelling. Brandon Lee was his son. Brandon Lee was also an actor. He was making a movie called *The Crow*. In one scene, an actor fires a gun at Lee. Lee then activates a switch hidden in his costume. He sets off a squib. Squibs are small exploding devices. They create special effects of getting shot. The bullets are supposed to be blank. Blanks have gunpowder. The bullets should have a cardboard tip instead of a metal tip. But the crew made a mistake. One of the bullets still had a metal tip. When the shot was fired, a real bullet hit Lee. Lee died at age 28. The film director finished the movie. He used a double for Lee. He also used special effects. Lee's death was a stunt accident. But some people think Lee and his father were a part of a curse.

Sound effects artists create sounds for fight scenes.
Some hit pumpkins. This makes a meaty, choppy sound.

CHAPTER 4

SOUND EFFECTS

Do you jump after hearing a loud sound? Sounds are important to movies. They help create the illusion. They make the scenes feel more real.

Sound effects artists want viewers to believe in the scene. They create sounds to match the actions of each scene. There are 4 main types of sound effects. Hard sound effects are common sounds. They include door alarms, punches, and cars driving by. Background sound effects are part of the **ambience**. Ambience means setting. These sounds include bird chirps. They include people talking or dogs barking. Electronic sound effects are made by a piano keyboard. They include laser blasts or spaceship hums. They're popular in science-fiction movies and video games.

TEST IT OUT!

Imagine making movies about fairies or giants. Movies can make tall people short. They can make short people tall. They do this by tricking the eyes. They distort the way something looks on screen. They use the science concept of forced perspective. Learn more about this movie magic trick.

Materials

- 2 objects like toys or chairs
- 2 friends
- Smartphone

1. Go outside. Look ahead. Everything you see is your visual field.

2. Pick something in the distance. Cover it up using your thumb. The distant object is larger than your thumb. But you're able to cover it with your thumb. Your thumb takes up the same amount of visual space as the large object in the distance. This is because your thumb is closer to your eye.

3. Place an object or a friend in your line of sight.

4. Open the camera app on a smartphone. Move closer to your object or friend. Observe what happens. The object or your friend takes up a larger amount of the camera's visual field. This makes the object or your friend appear bigger.

5. Now use 2 objects or 2 friends. Place one closer to your camera. Place the other further away. What do you observe?

Sound design effects are sounds that need to be created. Sound effects artists need to make unavailable sounds. This includes the sound of ships sinking. Sound effects artists need to make sounds of unreal objects. This includes monsters and aliens. For example, sound effects artists had to make sounds for The Child, or Baby Yoda, in *The Mandalorian*. They used a combination of sounds. They used noises from babies. They used noises from bat-eared foxes. They used noises from kinkajous.

Movie sounds aren't made during the filming. They're made in post-production. They're added after movies are filmed. This helps actors. It's distracting to film sounds in real time. Actors might miss their lines.

Sound effects artists use different props.
Props are objects used to make sounds.

Regular movies are 2-D. They're two-dimensional. They have length and width. Action is happening on the screen.

CHAPTER 5

3-D MOVIES

Have you ever been to a 3-D movie? 3-D movies make images look more lifelike. Viewers feel like they could walk right into the movie. They feel like they could reach out and touch objects.

3-D movies are an experience. Viewers can see different perspectives of an object. They see width. They see length. They see depth.

Humans have great depth **perception**. Perception is the ability to see. Your eyes are slightly set apart. Each eye has a slightly different perspective of what you're looking at. Your brain takes these images and creates depth. **Stereoscopy** is how your eyes and brain work together to see dimensions.

SCIENTIST SPOTLIGHT

Saugat Bista has a world record. He's the youngest film director. At age 7, he made a movie. His movie is called *Love You Baba*. It was filmed in Nepal, Asia. The movie was released in 2014. It's about a single father taking care of his daughter. It was shot in 27 days. Saugat directed how the film would be made. He chose the actors. He presented the movie's message. In 2018, he directed another movie. The movie is called *Hairaan*. Saugat said, "We are trying to present the story of characters who face several obstacles while going about their daily lives." Some of Saugat's family members are in the movie business. They taught him how to make movies. Before directing, Saugat acted in commercials and 2 films.

3-D moviemakers try to copy stereoscopy. They use special cameras. These are cameras that have 2 lenses. The lenses are like human eyes. The cameras create 2 versions of each image. Each image has a slightly different perspective. Both images are projected on a screen. Your eyes just need to merge the images. This is done with special glasses. These glasses help create the 3-D effect.

Today's 3-D glasses are **polarized**. Polarized means having different focus points. These glasses only allow a single image into each eye. Your brain joins the images together. This is how you see 3-D movies.

Older 3-D glasses had 2 different colors.

"Binge watching" TV shows was popularized by
Netflix, a major streaming service.

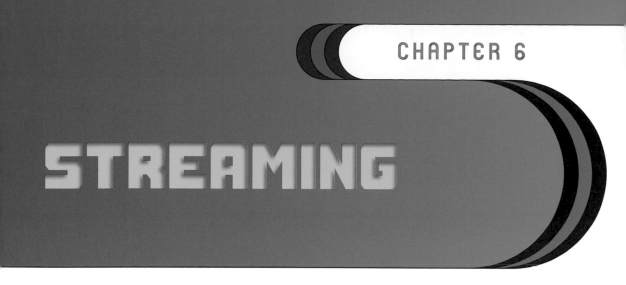

CHAPTER 6

STREAMING

Do you watch movies at home or on your phone? Many people have devices connected to the internet. You can **stream** movies. Streaming is the continuous **transmission** of files over the internet. Transmission is the act of sending signals. You can stream **audio**, or sound, files through platforms like Spotify or Pandora. You can stream video files through platforms like Netflix or YouTube.

Streaming is different from **downloading**. Downloading means copying and storing files. It takes longer. Streaming loads a little bit at a time. Streaming files are transmitted a few seconds at a time over the internet.

Streaming first became popular in 2005.
YouTube made it popular.

Internet speed is important when streaming. It's more important than accuracy. When streaming, not every **pixel** needs to be present in every frame. Pixel means a picture element. It's a small point in an image. Viewers would prefer to watch in normal speed. They don't want to wait for every bit of data to be delivered. So, a few lost data bits are okay.

Sometimes, internet connections are disrupted. But streaming video and audio files can keep playing. This is because of **buffering**. Buffering happens when a video or audio file pauses in order to download more data. It allows videos to play smoothly. Over slow connections, videos could take a while to buffer.

GLOSSARY

ambience (AM-bee-uhns) the character and atmosphere of a place

animated (AN-i-may-tid) a type of movie in which drawings are made to appear as moving images

audio (AW-dee-oh) sound

body doubles (BOD-ee DUH-buhls) stunt actors who serve as stand-ins for movie stars

buffering (BUH-fuhr-ing) downloading a certain amount of data before starting to play the music or movie

computer-generated (kuhm-PYOO-tur JEN-uh-ray-tuhd) using computer graphics to create or add to images in movies

downloading (DOWN-loh-ding) receiving, copying, and storing files from a remote system

graphics (GRAF-iks) images

illusion (i-LOO-zhuhn) misleading image

perception (pur-SEP-shuhn) the ability to see

pixel (PIK-suhl) a picture element that is the smallest point in an image

polarized (POH-luh-ryzd) having different focus points

post-production (POHST pruh-DUHK-shuhn) the time period after a movie is done being filmed, in which it is edited and prepared for release

production (pruh-DUHK-shuhn) the time period in which a movie is filmed

stereoscopy (ster-ee-AH-skuh-pee) a technique used to enable a 3-D effect

stream (STREEM) continuous transmission of audio or video files

stunts (STUHNTZ) daring feats

superimpose (soo-puhr-im-POHZ) to layer on top of something

textures (TEKS-churz) how things feel

three-dimensional (THREE-dai-MEN-shuh-nuhl) having length, width, and depth

transmission (transs-MISH-uhn) the act of sending electrical signals

LEARN MORE

Farrell, Dan, and Donna Bamford. *The Movie Making Book: Skills and Projects to Learn and Share*. Chicago, IL: Chicago Review Press, 2017.

Herman, Sarah. *Brick Flicks: A Comprehensive Guide to Making Your Own Stop-Motion LEGO Movies*. New York, NY: Skyhorse, 2014.

Loh-Hagan, Virginia. *Sound Effects Artist*. Ann Arbor, MI: Cherry Lake Publishing, 2016.

Roussos, Eleni. *The Moviemaking Magic of Marvel Studios: Heroes & Villains*. New York, NY: Abrams Books for Young Readers, 2019.

INDEX

ambience, 21

background sound effects, 21
belief, suspending, 15
Bista, Saugat, 26
body doubles, 17, 19
brain, 11, 25, 27
buffering, 31

cameras, 5–6, 10, 22, 27
CGI (computer-generated imagery), 12–15, 16, 18
colors, 14, 15

data, 28, 31
depth perception, 25
details, 15
digital video, 14
dimensions, 25
DLP technology, 14
downloading, 29

editing software, 14
electronic sound effects, 21
eyes, 11, 25, 27

film director, 26
forced perspective, 22

glasses, 3-D, 27
graphics, computer, 13, 15

hard sound effects, 21

illusions, 11, 21
images, misleading, 11
internet, 14, 29, 31

Lee, Bruce and Brandon, 19
lighting, 6, 14, 15

make-up, 14
models, 9, 13
movies
    introduction, 4–7
    types of, 5
    unsolved mystery, 19
    weird science, 14
    why people watch them, 5

Netflix, 29

perception, 25
perspective, 22, 27
pixels, 31
post-production work, 18, 23
production, 18
projectors, 14
props, 23

reels, 14

safety gear, 18
signals, 29
sound design effects, 23
sound effects, 20–23
special effects, 19
squibs, 19
stereoscopy, 25, 27
still images, 9
stop-motion, 8–11, 12
streaming, 28–31
stunts, 6, 16–18, 19

texture, 15
3-D models, 13
3-D movies, 24–27
transmission, 29

Wizard of Oz, 14

YouTube, 29, 30